TO COOPER GOLDMAN

I give special thanks to the extraordinarily helpful Wyeth Estate and the Brandywine River Museum. I particularly want to express my gratitude to Karen Baumgartner, Mary Beth Dolan, and Bethany Engel. They gave me the benefit of their deep knowledge. All factual material in this book has been checked in detail and confirmed by representatives of the three artists: N.C. Wyeth, Andrew Wyeth, and Jamie Wyeth. Any mistakes are my own. I also want to thank my editor, Victoria Rock, her assistant, Taylor Norman, and the talented designer Kayla Ferriera for making this book possible. And a huge thank-you to George Nicholson and his assistant Caitlin McDonald.

Library of Congress Cataloging-in-Publication Data:

Rubin, Susan Goldman.
Everybody paints! : the lives and art of the Wyeth family /
by Susan Goldman Rubin. — 1st [edition].
pages cm
ISBN 978-0-8118-6984-3 (alk. paper)
1. Wyeth family—Juvenile literature. 2. Artists—United States—Biography—Juvenile literature. I. Title.

N6537.W85R83 2013
759.13—dc23
[B]
2013006595

Manufactured in China.

Design by Kayla Ferriera.
Typeset in Archer, Brandon Grotesque, and Foundry Wilson.

10 9 8 7 6 5 4 3 2

Chronicle Books LLC
680 Second Street, San Francisco, California 94107

Chronicle Books—we see things differently.
Enjoy our publishing and become part of our community at www.chroniclekids.com.

The Lives and Art *of the* Wyeth Family

EVERYBODY PAINTS!

BY SUSAN GOLDMAN RUBIN

chronicle books·san francisco

Author's Note

This is the story of a unique family of artists: Newell Convers (N.C.) Wyeth, his son Andrew, and Andrew's son James, nicknamed Jamie—three generations of painters. I viewed their collective work on a trip to Maine when I visited the Wyeth Center at the Farnsworth Art Museum.

How did one family produce such extraordinary art?

N.C., the greatest American illustrator of the early twentieth century, encouraged Andrew and his siblings to draw. "*Drawing*!" N.C. wrote to his mother. "That's the outstanding stunt in this house."

Later Andrew said, "It was the most imaginative, rich childhood you could ever want. That's why I have so much inside of me that I want to paint."

Like his sisters Henriette and Carolyn, Andrew studied art with their father at home in Chadds Ford, Pennsylvania. All three became professional painters. Andrew's son Jamie followed family tradition. As a boy Jamie studied drawing and painting with his aunt Carolyn right in his legendary grandfather's studio.

When I toured the studio as part of my visit to the Brandywine River Museum, I saw unfinished paintings on the easels, frames hanging from the rafters, and streaks of paint still on the floor, just the way the Wyeths had left it.

"Everybody in my family paints," Jamie has said, "excluding possibly the dogs."

CONTENTS

CHAPTER 1
THE LITTLE FELLER
Page 8

CHAPTER 2
BRONCO BUSTER
Page 12

CHAPTER 3
RIDING THE RANGE
Page 16

CHAPTER 4
TREASURE ISLAND
Page 20

CHAPTER 5
ON ROCKY HILL
Page 24

CHAPTER 6
ALWAYS ROBIN HOOD
Page 30

CHAPTER 7
HOLIDAY MAGIC
Page 38

CHAPTER 8
SCRATCHES AND SPIT
Page 42

CHAPTER 9
JUST LIKE BLUEBERRIES
Page 50

CHAPTER 10
ONE SUMMER IN MAINE
Page 58

CHAPTER 11
DANGEROUS AND LOOMING
Page 66

CHAPTER 12
GHOST OF N.C. WYETH
Page 72

CHAPTER 13
PORTRAITS
Page 78

CHAPTER 14
WOLF DOG
Page 88

CHAPTER 15
ILLUSTRATING MY LIFE
Page 96

ARTWORK LOCATIONS
Page 101

IMAGE CREDITS
Page 102

BIBLIOGRAPHY
Page 103

INDEX
Page 104

THE LITTLE FELLER

When N.C. Wyeth was born, his parents couldn't agree on a name, so for the first two weeks of his life they called him "the little feller." His mother wanted to name him after her father. But his father wanted to combine two names from his family, Newell and Convers, and he won. "Papa's word and way held sway," N.C.'s mother said.

The oldest of four children, Newell Convers, later called N.C., was born in Needham, Massachusetts, on October 22, 1882. He and his mother would always feel especially close. His father, known as Newell, owned a grain business. Every day Newell left for work early in the morning and returned home late in the evening. He even worked on Sundays, so N.C. hardly saw him.

As a boy N.C. took charge of his younger brothers, Nathaniel, Edwin, and Stimson. Under his leadership they went canoeing on the Charles River, ice-skating when the river froze, and played football and baseball.

From early childhood N.C. had "a constant urge to draw." He set up a drawing table in a corner of his bedroom and created a little studio. His first pictures were of his house, his mother, their cow, and his pony, Bud.

At the one-room school he attended, he filled the margins of his textbooks with more drawings. Although he didn't like schoolwork, he loved

N.C. WYETH, *JIM HAWKINS LEAVES HOME* FROM *TREASURE ISLAND*, 1911, OIL ON CANVAS

his teacher. "Study nature, not books," was her motto, inspiring in N.C.
a love of the outdoors.

When he started attending Needham High School at age twelve, he
hated it. So at age fifteen N.C. announced that he was going to drop out of
school to train as an artist. He had taken a few art lessons from a neighbor.
Now he wanted more.

His father was appalled. He considered an artist to be "someone un-
kempt, . . . living a disordered life, not earning enough to support himself."
Newell decided that N.C. should spend a year working as a farmhand to
knock "this artist nonsense out of his head."

N.C. refused.

His mother took his side. She brought his drawings to Boston and showed
them to a few art instructors. They agreed that N.C. had talent. They recom-
mended he attend the Mechanic Arts High School, where in addition to basic
drawing he would learn drafting, which he could use as an architect or engineer. N.C.'s mother convinced his father that at art school their son would learn
practical skills for a trade. So in the fall N.C. began commuting to Boston.

N.C. studied at the Mechanic Arts High School for two years. When he
graduated, at age seventeen, he still dreamed of being an artist, but he knew
he needed more training. "Art is a thing that has to be studied right," he
said. So he asked his father for a loan to pay his tuition at the Massachusetts
Normal Arts School, also in Boston. His father agreed and N.C. vowed to
someday pay him back.

One of N.C.'s teachers suggested that he had the talent to become
an illustrator. "And right there," said N.C., "I jumped at a straw." He set

his goal on "painting pictures good enough to be used in *Scribner's*," his favorite magazine.

In those days, the early 1900s, before television and computers, people got much of their information and entertainment from magazines. Popular magazines such as *Scribner's Monthly*, *Collier's Weekly,* and *The Saturday Evening Post* were illustrated with wonderful paintings, and the illustrators who created these images earned huge sums of money.

N.C. knew he wanted to become an illustrator, yet his classes in anatomy and perspective bored him. Then one day a friend came back from the Howard Pyle School of Art in Wilmington, Delaware, and raved about it. Pyle was considered one of the greatest illustrators of his day. He had written and illustrated books for children such as *The Merry Adventures of Robin Hood*, as well as depicting historical events for adults in books and magazines. At the height of his success, he had opened a school. He accepted only twelve students at a time, regarding them as apprentices in the art of picture making.

N.C. gathered up his courage and submitted his drawings to Pyle, hoping that he would be chosen. Pyle thought N.C.'s drawings were "very promising." Although N.C. was not accepted as one of the twelve full-time students, Pyle invited him to come to Wilmington to attend his weekly lectures on composition.

So in 1902, the day after his twentieth birthday, N.C. left home with his gripsack and portfolio. His mother was heartbroken to see him go and gave in to "fits of crying." N.C. would later capture the emotion of their parting in an illustration for *Treasure Island* that shows young Jim, the hero of the book, leaving home as his mother weeps into her apron.

CHAPTER
2

BRONCO BUSTER

With great expectations, N.C. went to Pyle's house. He thrilled at meeting "the master." "Just think," he wrote to his mother, "Me—seeing Pyle himself and his original works."

N.C. showed Pyle some new sketches, still hoping to be accepted as an apprentice. N.C. had heard that Pyle kept applicants guessing, so his hopes soared when Pyle told him to send for his collection of costumes, guns, and reference books.

N.C. was eager to start working as an illustrator. "I wish I could earn a living now," he wrote to his parents. "I know that there are three more [brothers] to prepare for life and it makes me feel that it's not right for me here spending money." Not to mention, he wanted to prove to his father that an artist could earn a good income.

In his room at the boardinghouse where he was staying, N.C. immediately started drawing. Then he held his breath in anticipation of receiving his first critique at Pyle's weekly lecture. Pausing at N.C.'s sketch, Pyle pointed out that N.C.'s drawing had exciting action and a good composition. N.C. was encouraged and turned in another drawing the next week.

A fellow student introduced N.C. to Guernsey Moore, an editor at *The Saturday Evening Post*. Moore praised N.C.'s drawings and suggested that N.C. try a Western theme for his next batch of illustrations.

N.C. WYETH, *CUTTING OUT (COLORADO)*, 1904, OIL ON CANVAS

Back in his room, N.C. worked feverishly. At Pyle's next lecture he submitted his drawing of a cowboy riding a bucking bronco. To everyone's amazement, Pyle told N.C. to take the drawing to Moore the very next morning. Moore "went wild over" the picture and offered him $60 for it, the equivalent of more than $1,000 today. The picture, *Bronco Buster*, appeared on the cover of the February 21, 1903 issue of *The Saturday Evening Post*. It was N.C.'s first published illustration. As soon as the magazine hit the newsstands, Pyle summoned N.C. to his house and officially accepted him as a fullfledged student. However, there was one condition: N.C. had to stop painting pictures for magazines and devote himself to formal training. Pyle promised N.C. that if he did this, at the end of his studies he would have more commissions than he had ever dreamed of.

So N.C. began with fundamentals, drawing from plaster casts and painting in black and white to learn about light and shadow. Pyle kept strict working hours for himself and his students. In the morning, N.C. and the others drew from costumed models, and in the afternoon, from memory. Pyle arrived late in the day to give critiques.

"Pictures are creations of imagination," he said to his students. "Live in your picture. Dig deep."

N.C. worked at an easel in one of three studios. Natural light poured through the skylight. N.C. and the other students dressed like Pyle in dark suits, starched shirts, and neckties. Because N.C. was Pyle's favorite student and about the same size, Pyle occasionally gave him his hand-me-downs. Once he gave him a dress suit so that N.C. would have the proper clothes for attending a formal dance.

In the summer N.C. and the students moved to Pyle's summer house in Chadds Ford, Pennsylvania, eleven miles away. N.C. loved it there.

The rolling farmland of the Brandywine Valley reminded him of home. He drew and painted outdoors, and Pyle praised his work as "the *strongest*, most *practical* and on the whole the *best* of all."

Yet back in the Wilmington studio, N.C. struggled to achieve the artistic level of his *Saturday Evening Post* cover. After one of Pyle's critiques, N.C. wrote to his mother, "People can talk about art being a 'dead cinch' but they are mightily mistaken. It's grind, grind, grind all the time, from early until late."

By the winter of 1904, however, N.C. had advanced to the top of his class. Unlike some artists who longed to study in Europe, he knew he wanted to stay in America and paint American subjects. N.C. planned on returning to Needham and establishing a studio there. But that winter his plans changed.

RIDING THE RANGE

In the winter of 1904, N.C. went to a sleighing party and was smitten by a beauty named Carolyn Bockius, nicknamed Carol. Carol was eighteen years old, shy, and slender. At six foot one and weighing two hundred pounds, N.C. towered over her.

Pyle didn't approve of this blossoming romance. "Art and marriage won't mix," he said. N.C. felt torn. He respected Pyle and wanted to please him, but he cared about Carol.

In the spring N.C. heard that Joseph Chapin, the famed art editor of Scribner's, a publisher of books as well as the magazine, wanted to meet with him. N.C. hurried to New York City and Chapin gave him a manuscript to consider right on the spot. His dream of illustrating for *Scribner's Magazine* was on the verge of becoming a reality, but N.C. didn't feel that the story, a historical romance, was suited to his art style, so he regretfully turned down the project. Chapin, impressed by N.C.'s honesty, offered him another manuscript. This one appealed to N.C., so he accepted the assignment. His first book illustration was published the following November.

Meanwhile, N.C. continued to court Carol. He took her walking through fields in Chadds Ford and paddling on the Brandywine River in his birchbark canoe. As they spent more and more time together, their feelings for each other deepened.

PHOTOGRAPH OF N.C. WYETH ON HORSEBACK, 1904

The students at Pyle's school never knew how long their studies would last: There was no set graduation. Only Pyle decided when each had finished training. On August 12, 1904, Pyle informed N.C. that he had officially graduated. He suggested N.C. take a trip to the American West to inspire his painting. N.C. liked the idea. He already sported a big Stetson hat. *Scribner's* agreed to pay N.C.'s travel expenses on the condition that N.C. allow them the opportunity to publish his Western paintings before N.C. offered them to any other magazines.

In October 1904, just before his twenty-second birthday, N.C. left for cattle country near Denver, Colorado. Although he had planned on simply sketching a roundup, he actually took part in it. For two weeks N.C. rode the range, herding cattle and roping horses. "I feel perfectly at home here," he wrote to Carol.

When the roundup was done, N.C. rented a studio in Denver and began painting from his sketches. For the first time, N.C. was painting on his own without the benefit of comments from his teacher or classmates. *Was his work any good?* he wondered. He finished four canvases and was about to pack them up when a Denver businessman visited his studio and offered to buy the whole set. The offer boosted N.C.'s confidence, but he refused to sell the paintings, honoring his pledge to *Scribner's*.

In November N.C. traveled to Arizona and sketched on a Navajo reservation. Then he crossed the Rockies and rode to New Mexico. He had put his savings in a government trading post in Muddy Springs, New Mexico, but Mexican bandits raided the post and stole all the money. N.C. joined a posse to track them down. They never found the thieves. N.C. took a job delivering mail on horseback to earn enough money for his trip home.

He reached home just before Christmas in 1904. He and Carol had exchanged love letters during his travels. That December they became secretly engaged. N.C.'s parents had feared that Carol would distract him from his work. But when he gave his father the news about the engagement, his father was "very much pleased." His mother, however, acted cold and withheld congratulations.

Pyle, on the other hand, had changed his mind; he had come to appreciate Carol's influence on N.C. Pyle eagerly reviewed N.C.'s Western paintings and suggested that he write an article about his adventures to go with them. *Scribner's* loved the whole project and published N.C.'s article, "A Day with the Round-Up," illustrated by his paintings.

N.C. quickly became known for his images of the American West and was flooded with fan mail and commissions from all over the country. Pyle's prediction had come true: N.C. had more work than he had ever imagined, and he felt ready to leave the security of Pyle's studio. Luckily a former student of Pyle's had built a group of studios for Pyle's students to use when they started off on their own. Soon N.C. was earning enough money to repay the loan from his father. Just as importantly, he was finally earning enough money to take care of himself and a wife.

On April 16, 1906, N.C. and Carol were married. They had no honeymoon because N.C. was too busy filling orders for pictures.

"Gee! It's pouring in," he wrote to his parents. "I hope something won't bust."

TREASURE ISLAND

Despite N.C.'s success as an illustrator, he felt dissatisfied. "If only someday I can be called a *painter*!" he wrote to his mother. He felt his illustrations were a lesser form of art "than paintings that lived on their own, not tied to a book." N.C. struggled to be recognized as a painter, not an illustrator, and was tempted to give up his commercial work. Yet he needed to keep doing illustrations for magazines and advertisements in order to support his family. N.C.'s son Andrew was later to say that N.C.'s illustrations were his best work. "*No one* else could have ever done them but him," said Andrew. "He never got the excitement out of a landscape that he got when he painted from his imagination."

In December 1906, Carol gave birth to their first child, a daughter named Carolyn. The baby died five days later. N.C. and Carol were overcome with grief. But soon Carol became pregnant again, and their second baby was born on October 22, 1907, N.C.'s twenty-fifth birthday. They named their daughter Ann Henriette for her two grandmothers. "My heart has gone out to her completely," N.C. wrote to his mother.

Happy in his family life, yet still disappointed in his art, in spring of 1908 N.C. decided he would "paint only for myself." He and Carol rented a house in Chadds Ford so N.C. could focus on painting landscapes.

They both loved the country. "I feel as though I could eat the dirt, it is so honest and wholesome!" wrote N.C. In the morning he drew and

N.C. WYETH, ENDPAPER ILLUSTRATION FOR *TREASURE ISLAND*, 1911, OIL ON CANVAS

painted outdoors. After lunch he cranked out pictures for *Scribner's* and *The Saturday Evening Post*. Then he did more painting. At night he, Carol, and the baby swung in a hammock on the porch, gazing at the stars.

Although N.C. judged his illustrations "flashy" and "superficial," orders piled in. Collectors wanted to buy the original paintings that had been reproduced in magazines. Four of his commercial paintings won first prize at a show at the Pennsylvania Academy of the Fine Arts. "But this does not mean much to me," he said. "How eager I am to paint paint paint!"

When the prestigious Macbeth Gallery in New York invited him to exhibit and sell his landscapes, he refused because he was still experimenting. "Wait until I do something *good*!!" he said.

N.C. read the book *Walden*. Its author, Henry David Thoreau, had written about his experience spending two years in a cabin in the woods, living a simple life close to nature. Inspired by Thoreau, and the beauty of Chadds Ford, N.C. kept painting landscapes, hoping this would be his finest work. Yet, with the birth of another baby named Carolyn, N.C. had to accept commercial assignments to earn money.

In February 1911, Scribner's asked him to illustrate an "elaborate edition" of *Treasure Island,* by Robert Louis Stevenson. The adventure story of Jim Hawkins and Long John Silver searching for buried treasure captivated N.C. And when his editor told him he'd be paid a fee of $2,500 (equal to more than $50,000 today), N.C. immediately accepted.

With the first installment of the money, N.C. bought eighteen acres of land on Rocky Hill, less than a mile from Chadds Ford. The wooded property had a brook and an orchard. Construction of a new house and studio began as he started work on the book.

Unlike earlier editions of the story, N.C. decided not to focus on the hero, but to illustrate the moments that lead up to the most important events in the book. Only six of the seventeen paintings feature the hero, Jim Hawkins. The rest of the scenes are shown from Jim's point of view, which N.C. believed would make the reader feel more involved in the action. "The reader is actually the boy at all times," said N.C., and "sees, hears, tastes, or smells nothing but what [Jim] did."

Excitedly, N.C. spent nine hours a day on the project, sometimes more. "Work is coming splendidly," he wrote. "I never felt so strong in my life." For each illustration he painted an enormous canvas nearly four feet high and more than three feet wide.

When N.C. sent the first group of paintings to Scribner's, his editor was ecstatic. "Pictures great," wired Chapin in a telegram. N.C. finished the last paintings in a burst of energy. On July 26, he wrote, "*Treasure Island* completed! . . . I've turned out a set of pictures, without doubt far better in quality than anything I ever did . . . with regret I packed the last canvas in the big box tonight. I so thoroughly enjoyed the work."

The book was published on October 22, 1911, N.C.'s twenty-ninth birthday. The first edition of the book sold out by December 18, and a second printing, ready in time for Christmas, sold out too. With *Treasure Island* N.C. became known as the foremost book illustrator of his day.

Two days after the book was published, Carol gave birth to a son. In the begining, the family called him Baby Brother. He was later named Nathanial and nicknamed Nat because N.C. noticed that he was astonishingly like his own brother Nat. They were both fascinated with wheels and machinery.

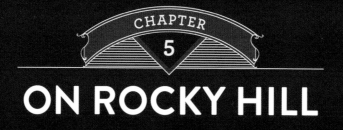

ON ROCKY HILL

After the publication of *Treasure Island*, N.C. plunged into one of his dark moods. In spite of the book's enormous success, N.C. had come to feel the illustrations were worthless. He said, "I never wanted to see or hear of the things again." Letters of praise irritated him. He thought that no one judged the work as truthfully as he did. When Scribner's asked him to illustrate another classic, he chose *Kidnapped,* by Robert Louis Stevenson, and vowed to do better. He said to his editor, "Unless I outclass *Treasure Island* I want you to cancel the entire scheme."

However, he took pleasure in painting the canvases that depict the adventures of young David Balfour, a Scottish orphan, who fights to claim his rightful inheritance. "I have thoroughly enjoyed doing the book, every minute of it," declared N.C., yet he wrote to his editor, "Now that the books are done I feel very eager to do some really *good* stuff."

Once again he turned to landscape painting as a "better" pursuit. But he continued to be unhappy with the results. "I am feeling utterly disgusted with my present attempts in the studio," he wrote. "I want to wipe the slate clean of everything but my family."

N.C. loved taking care of his children. They now lived in their new house on Rocky Hill. N.C. called it the Homestead. There, in the evening,

N.C. WYETH, *THE SIEGE OF THE ROUND-HOUSE* FROM *KIDNAPPED*, 1913, OIL ON CANVAS

he drew pictures of pirates and Indians and giants for the children, and they too drew for him. He fed and bathed them and put them to bed. Later he went from room to room checking on each child. Henriette, the oldest, said that he "took care of us like a great, wonderful nanny."

After the children were in bed, he would often fall asleep reading a manuscript he was preparing to illustrate. At dawn he would go to his studio to start a new composition. Then he'd hurry to the kitchen to make breakfast for everyone, waking up the household by banging loud chords on the piano. After breakfast he made sure that each child was happily occupied with an activity before going back to the studio and his own work.

In September 1914, war broke out in Europe and the famous newspaper publisher William Randolph Hearst asked N.C. to go overseas to sketch the fighting at the front. N.C. seriously considered the proposal. He had illustrated many battles for books. But he turned down Hearst's offer, saying, "There is nothing more interesting or important going on in those fields of carnage than what happens in this little house every hour."

In March 1915, another baby girl was born, and they named her Ann. "She interests me as an infant more than any of the others did," said N.C., "on account of her sense of humor." He called Ann "my joker."

N.C.'s sister-in-law Nancy came to live with them and help look after the Wyeth brood. For *Robin Hood* Nancy posed for the figure of Maid Marian because his wife, Carol, was happily pregnant again. But for the glowing face of Maid Marian, he painted Carol's portrait.

Although *Robin Hood* takes place in Sherwood Forest, England, N.C. depicted the Brandywine Valley as the setting. Robin Hood and his companions shoot arrows from a wooded slope on Rocky Hill.

N.C. WYETH, *ROBIN MEETS MAID MARIAN* FROM *ROBIN HOOD*, 1917, OIL ON CANVAS

That same year, the United States entered the war raging in Europe. The War Department offered N.C. a first lieutenant's commission to go overseas as a "war artist." Though honored and flattered, he refused. His wife and children, he said, needed him more than the U.S. Army. Still, N.C. took time out from illustrating to paint posters for the Red Cross and the U.S. Navy. He didn't like what he produced and said, "I'll be glad when my share of this work is done."

For his next classic, *The Boy's King Arthur*, N.C. used the landscape of Rocky Hill again. The British armored knights battling in the scene titled, *They Fought with Him on Foot More than Three Hours, Both Before and Behind Him*, actually clang swords on a spring afternoon in Pennsylvania. By using his contemporary environment, N.C. brought the pictures to life. He said he was painting figures "in the light and air as you see and breathe it."

On July 12, 1917, Carol gave birth to a baby boy. N.C. was especially thrilled because that day was the hundredth anniversary of the birth of his hero, Henry David Thoreau. They named the baby Andrew Newell Wyeth III. N.C. said the baby was "lively as a cricket."

The girls called their brother "Andy Pandy." Their grandmother called him "my little snowdrop." Henriette, age ten, stared at Andrew's face and said, "He looks as though he's going to be a great composer or artist."

She was right.

N.C. WYETH, *THEY FOUGHT WITH HIM ON FOOT MORE THAN THREE HOURS, BOTH BEFORE HIM AND BEHIND HIM* FROM *THE BOY'S KING ARTHUR*, 1917, OIL ON CANVAS

ALWAYS ROBIN HOOD

Andrew and Ann were called the "youngers." Their older brother, Nat,
constructed a toy barn for them, and together Andrew and Ann built
adjoining farms on the floor of the basement playroom. "I loved it that I
played with . . . this miniature world," said Andrew. "I wanted to create
this thing and *use* it, let my imagination go."

Ann loved dolls but Andrew's favorites were trains, a hook and ladder
that pumped real water, and his toy soldiers. When he was six, N.C. painted
his portrait. Andrew wouldn't hold still. N.C. gave him the toy fire engine
to hold, but he kept moving, so N.C. left the hands unfinished.

Andrew spent hours making up games with his toy soldiers. He named
the soldiers and drew pictures of them. "I built my own stories, and that is
the way painting has been to me," he recalled. Years later, as an adult, he
remained fascinated by World War I and painted a portrait, *The German*, of
his neighbor Karl Kuerner wearing his old war helmet. Karl and his wife
Anna had settled on a farm in Chadds Ford, and Andrew liked to wander
over there and listen to Karl's tales about battles and watch Anna raking
and doing chores. Andrew was to draw and paint at the Kuerners' farm for
more than fifty years.

PHOTOGRAPH OF WYETH CHILDREN, 1919, TAKEN BY N.C. WYETH.
FROM LEFT TO RIGHT: **ANN HOLDING A DOLL, NAT, BABY ANDREW IN
HENRIETTE'S ARMS, AND CAROLYN**

Growing up, all of the Wyeth children enjoyed drawing. "If you didn't draw," said Henriette, "that was like turning down bread and butter and milk and not eating anything."

N.C. wrote, "To see the whole five around the lamp at night, bent over a tablet of paper, recording all sorts of facts and fictions of nature, one would at least guess it were an organized night art school."

Henriette drew fairy-tale pictures of girls and angels and blossoms. When she was eleven, N.C. took her into his studio and began giving her academic instruction. "Henriette's natural ability to draw is so astonishing that I hardly know what to do about it," he wrote to his mother. Later, when Henriette was fourteen, she went to the same art school in Boston that N.C. had attended.

Nat drew little pictures in tight squares, but he was more interested in taking apart things like alarm clocks or designing and building model boats. N.C. realized that Nat was a born engineer and gave him tools and explained how they worked.

Carolyn skillfully sketched horses. She loved animals and had dogs, a pony named Taboo, and a pet rooster. N.C. began giving her formal art lessons as an apprentice when she was twelve. For the next four years he kept her drawing spheres, cones, and plaster busts in charcoal.

Andrew considered himself the least gifted. However, he was the most dedicated. By the time he was six he was drawing constantly, staying up late with a pad on his knees in the playroom or on the windowsill of the bedroom he shared with Nat.

N.C. recorded Andrew's obsession in a huge picture titled *In A Dream I Meet General Washington*. In the painting Washington, on horseback,

N.C. WYETH, *IN A DREAM I MEET GENERAL WASHINGTON*, 1930–31, OIL ON CANVAS

turns to tell N.C. about the Battle of the Brandywine taking place behind
him. Young Andrew, in the foreground with a sketchpad on his knee, pays
no attention. N.C. said, "Here I am talking to Washington, a battle going on,
and Andy was just interested in drawing."

"I always showed him [N.C.] my work," recalled Andrew, "but not until
it was finished." N.C. talked to him seriously as though he were an adult art
student. "He had a marvelous way of never talking down to a young person,"
said Andrew. "That's a good start," N.C. might tell him. Or looking at a drawing of soldiers he would say, "Now, Andy, he wouldn't hold a rifle that way,"
and he'd draw it correctly in a corner of the page.

Andrew often went to his father's studio and rummaged through the
cupboard full of World War I memorabilia. He looked through the images
N.C. had painted to illustrate various books. Then he'd haul out a finished
canvas, almost as big as he was, and lug it over to the easel where N.C. was
painting, and ask questions. "My relationship with my father was different
from the rest of the children," said Andrew. "It was through his illustrations.
I fed on them."

As a boy Andrew was sensitive, nervous, and thin. He had a hip condition and wasn't athletic. When he started first grade, he hated it.

"The long days just about killed me," he said. So his parents took him
out and had him tutored at home. N.C. didn't think much of school anyway.
"No top-notch artist ever graduated from college," he said. The only one of
the Wyeth children who had a conventional education was Nat, who wanted
to become an engineer.

The girls were also tutored at home and read avidly. Funny papers
were banned, but books were treasured. N.C. lovingly painted *Portrait of
Ann Reading*. But Andrew was a restless student. During his mornings of

tutoring, he would glance longingly at his shelf of toy soldiers. Once he tricked his tutor into leaving early by turning the clock ahead. "I didn't even know my ABCs!" he said.

When Andrew was six, a new student arrived to study with N.C. The young man, age twenty, was named Peter Hurd. Andrew adored Peter, as did everyone else in the family. Once Peter asked Andrew to look something up in the encyclopedia. Peter was astounded that Andrew didn't know how to read, so he taught him. He also gave him a fountain pen in a little case just like his own to hang around his neck. Until then Andrew had been experimenting with pen points inserted in wooden penholders. "Even when I was little," said Andrew, "I was sensitive to the tools I used."

Because Andrew didn't go to school, he had few friends. "I felt so left out from other kids!" he said. "Paint was my only point, my only chance." His best pals were his sister Ann, his red Irish setter, Sanco, and a neighborhood boy, David Lawrence.

With Ann and David he'd dress up in costumes stored in his father's studio and act out the stories. "Andy was the smallest and he always took the best part and got the best costume," remembered Ann. "He was always Robin Hood." A photograph shows him in his tights and cape, with David at his side as Friar Tuck. Nat made wooden swords for the Merry Men. "We looked like the figures out of Howard Pyle and N.C. Wyeth," said Andrew. At the end of the day, the other kids would drift away, but he stayed in character. "To me it was sort of like building a painting."

N.C. WYETH, *PORTRAIT OF ANN READING*, 1930, OIL ON CANVAS

HOLIDAY MAGIC

N.C.'s life "revolved around children," said Andrew. "He loved our imagination and it excited him." N.C. made miraculous things happen for the holidays.
On Halloween he surprised the children with carved jack-o'-lanterns. Then
the whole family dressed up in masks and costumes from his studio and
went "haunting." To Andrew, Halloween had "the eerie feeling of another
world." The excitement and delicious terror of that night stayed with him as
an adult, and inspired a painting of carved pumpkins titled *Jack-Be-Nimble*.
His son Jamie embraced the Wyeth Halloween tradition in his spooky painting *Pumpkinhead-Self-Portrait*.

But when Andrew was a boy, the highlight of the year came at Christmas. On Christmas Eve the Wyeth children hung their stockings on their
bedposts. At 4:30 in the morning they heard the stamping of boots on the
roof and the ringing of sleigh bells. "I could almost hear the sound of sleigh
runners on the snow," recalled Andrew. He would get so excited that sometimes he would wet his bed. Then a booming voice told the reindeer to quiet
down. N.C. would appear dressed up as Old Kriss Kringle in a padded Eskimo
costume, a peaked red hat, and a long white beard. He filled the stockings and
shook hands with every child except Andrew, who was so scared he crawled
under the covers. "Old Kriss was horrifying. But magic," said Andrew.

LEFT: **ANDREW WYETH,** *JACK-BE-NIMBLE*, 1976, WATERCOLOR ON PAPER
RIGHT: **JAMIE WYETH,** *PUMPKINHEAD-SELF-PORTRAIT*, 1972, OIL ON CANVAS

A few minutes later N.C. would reappear as himself. Then just before dawn the children would scamper downstairs to behold the Christmas tree aglow with flickering candles. N.C. made them wait a minute to take in the beauty of the scene. Then they rushed to unwrap their presents, which were nearly always handmade. One year Nat constructed a fancy medieval castle for Andrew and N.C. painted the stonework, complete with vines creeping along the towers. Another time Nat and N.C. made doll furniture for Ann's collection. Each year Ann received a new doll from her mother. Once Carolyn got a pair of doves caged in a box that was painted silver on the inside.

"It was a mad shambles," said Andrew, "shouts of enthusiasm, hills of wrapping paper, the dogs in it all, pulling." Later on he would lie under the tree, gazing up at the angel, smelling the fragrant scent of pine. Henriette once said of Andrew, "He has never lost that Christmas-morning excitement."

The memory of Christmas strongly influenced Andrew's painting. "It's in my feelings for certain colors," he said, "the tans, the color of reindeer. It's in the strange mood of a landscape, that quality of Christmas Eve night."

N.C. WYETH, *OLD KRIS*, 1925, OIL ON CANVAS

SCRATCHES AND SPIT

By the time Andrew was ten he knew that painting would be his life's work. "Art seemed to be inside me," he said.

He spent hours drawing pictures of knights, pirates, soldiers, and cowboys. He copied drawings from art books. Andrew loved the work of Howard Pyle, who had been N.C.'s teacher, and he idolized Albrecht Dürer, an early-sixteenth-century artist who had done realistic studies of rabbits, plants, bugs, and people.

When Andrew was thirteen, N.C. gave him his first watercolor set, and he began painting watercolor landscapes in the orchard behind N.C.'s studio. At first he was timid and slow. N.C. said to him, "Andy, you want to explode on the thing." And he demonstrated by doing "part of the sky very quickly, with great bravado."

In October 1932, when Andrew was fifteen years old, N.C. took him into his studio to begin formal art lessons. He said to Andrew, "If you're not better than I am, I'm a rotten teacher."

Like Carolyn before him, Andrew started by drawing cubes, spheres, and pyramids with charcoal. "It was a terrible shock to me," he said, "because I wanted to *express* myself. Sitting down and drawing cubes drove me up a tree.

ANDREW WYETH, *CASTLE SIEGE*, 1932, PEN AND INK ON PAPER

But my father believed in it and I believed in it. You have to know the rules in order to break them."

For months Andrew did pencil drawings of a skeleton in various positions. Then, from memory, he had to show the skeleton walking. Next N.C. promoted Andrew to oil paint and had him do still lifes of coffeepots and apples. He hired local men to pose for portraits. "He was tough on me," said Andrew, "but I think he was right. If severe training kills an artist's ability, then it ought to be killed."

At that time a young man named John McCoy was studying with N.C. N.C. staged competitions in the studio between Andrew and John. They painted the same subject, and N.C. judged whose work was better.

John was dating Andrew's sister Ann. She had become serious about music and not only played the piano but also composed music. She and John soon became engaged, but N.C. wanted her to continue her musical training before getting married. In December 1934 her composition *A Christmas Fantasy* was performed by the Philadelphia Orchestra.

Henriette had also married one of N.C.'s students, Peter Hurd. Most of the year they lived and painted in the schoolhouse at the corner of the property that N.C. had bought for them, and they spent summers in New Mexico. Henriette had become a portrait painter, but she still brought her work to her father for criticism. Often his critique made her cry. Once he took her brush and repainted the whole background of a painting that she had thought was her best work. "But he was always right," she said.

N.C. never lectured about technique such as how to paint a tree or a head of hair. He talked about light, mood, drama. He told Carolyn, who

studied with him for nineteen years, "Never paint the material of the sleeve. *Become* the arm."

After two years of study, Andrew, at age seventeen, "graduated" from N.C.'s studio. Worried that Andrew wouldn't be able to earn a living as a fine artist, N.C. pushed him toward illustrating. At that time, 1934, the country was plunged in the Great Depression. Millions of Americans had no jobs, no homes, no money. But luckily for N.C., his artwork was still in demand. His earnings grew as assignments rolled in for painting murals as well as book and magazine illustrations.

PHOTOGRAPH OF ANDREW WYETH PAINTING AT HIS EASEL, C.1935

N.C. bought a four-door Cadillac, and hired a cook, butler, and maid. He built a tennis court behind the studio. And in 1920, he had purchased an old sea captain's house called Eight Bells in Port Clyde, Maine, where the family spent their summers.

When N.C. received a contract to illustrate Thoreau's *Men of Concord*, he let Andrew do the pen-and-ink work. But the book was published under N.C.'s name. In spring 1936, Andrew agreed to illustrate a book, but he found the story the publisher sent him was dull. What he really wanted to do was to go to Maine and paint watercolors. That night he went to bed thinking about the book and wondering what to do with it. N.C. must have realized how Andrew felt. In the morning he said, "Andy, it's ridiculous for you to

PHOTOGRAPH OF N.C. WYETH WEARING WHITE KNICKERS
AND A JACKET, STANDING IN FRONT OF HIS CADILLAC, 1928

do that book. Turn it down and go to Maine. I will support you. Go up there and paint like hell."

Andrew did. He drove up to Maine with his bull terrier, Lupe, and spent hours painting on the coast around Port Clyde. He carried his painting gear in a beat-up metal tackle box. He sat on the rocks, a sheet of custom-cut watercolor paper spread on his lap. The crashing waves exhilarated him. Watercolors felt like the right medium for capturing his "joyous excitement" and the wildness of the sea. "My best watercolors are when there's scratches and spit and mud, gobs of paint and crap over them," he said. "I never knew exactly what was going to happen." Sometimes he did eight paintings in a day and threw away as many as five.

When N.C. went up to Maine, he was amazed at Andrew's progress and predicted "big work ahead." He was right.

In the fall of 1936, the Philadelphia Art Alliance exhibited some of Andrew's watercolors. Not one of them sold. But after the exhibit closed Andrew took N.C.'s suggestion and dropped his paintings off at the Macbeth Gallery in New York City. The gallery was known for showing the work of important American artists such as Edward Hopper and Winslow Homer. Andrew soon received a letter from the gallery owner, Robert Macbeth, offering him a one-man show the following year.

The next summer Andrew returned to Maine to continue to improve his skill. The blueness of the bay and the lobstermen hauling traps inspired him. In the fall, after the rest of the family returned to Chadds Ford, Andrew sent his work to his father.

N.C. spread out the paintings and studied them. "They look *magnificent*," he wrote to Andrew. "They represent the *very best* watercolors I ever saw!"

Andrew replied, "What you had to say about my watercolors means more to me than you know. You are the only person that really understands what I am after."

On October 19, 1937, Andrew's show at the Macbeth Gallery opened. He was twenty years old. The whole Wyeth family attended the opening, except for Henriette and Peter, who had settled for good in faraway New Mexico. Because the country was in the midst of the Great Depression, Andrew didn't expect a big turnout. Only one painting sold that first night. However, unbeknownst to him, the art critic for *The New York Times* saw the show and wrote that Andrew's watercolors "bear evidence of a very real talent." And the critic for the *Herald Tribune* who was at the opening whispered to N.C., "Don't tell the boy, but let him read it in the paper that I think it's a corking show." The news spread.

The next day, on his way back to Chadds Ford, Andrew stopped at the gallery to see if anyone had visited his show. To his amazement both rooms were packed with people. "I nearly fainted," he said. Red foil stars indicating the paintings were sold gleamed on every frame. The show had totally sold out, a record for the gallery.

Andrew took the train back to Chadds Ford and N.C. met him at the station. N.C. was speechless. He took Andrew in his arms and hugged him. "What a welcome that was!" remembered Andrew.

But the next morning he was back in the studio studying anatomy.

ANDREW WYETH, *THE LOBSTERMAN,* **1937, WATERCOLOR ON PAPER**

CHAPTER 9

JUST LIKE BLUEBERRIES

Andrew felt that his successful watercolors were "too free, too deft, too popular." Later he dismissed this early work as his "blue sky" period.

N.C., however, realized that Andrew had established himself as a fine artist, a painter, a goal he had not yet achieved. "What magic power that boy has!" he wrote of Andrew's watercolors. "I am at once stimulated beyond words to new, purer effect, and plunged into black despair."

Andrew needed a new challenge and began experimenting with a different medium, tempera. A technique used by Renaissance artists, egg tempera is paint that is made from dry powder that is mixed with distilled water and an egg yolk. The paint has to be applied to a panel coated in gesso, a mixture of chalk and glue. Working in tempera requires slowly building up the surface, layering the paint "like a wasp's nest," said Andrew. He struggled with it for two years before mastering the technique.

Andrew's first tempera painting, done in 1936, featured his bull terrier, Lupe. Then he tried landscapes, portraits, and even self-portraits. In *The Revenant* he pictured himself as a person who returns as a spirit after death.

N.C. watched him and thought the results weren't colorful enough. "You won't sell any of those pictures," he said. Yet in a letter to Henriette, N.C. commented on Andrew's "truly remarkable temperas." He even tried

ANDREW WYETH, *THE REVENANT*, 1949, TEMPERA ON PANEL

N.C. WYETH, *ISLAND FUNERAL*, 1939, TEMPERA ON PANEL

the medium himself in a huge painting, four feet tall and almost five feet wide, titled *Island Funeral*. When the gallery owner Robert Macbeth visited the Wyeths in Maine the summer of 1939, he admired the painting and offered to exhibit it.

Andrew painted every day, but on July 12, his twenty-second birthday, he took a day off and went to visit Merle James, a newspaper editor he had met. James, nicknamed Jim, spent summers about fifteen miles away. When Andrew knocked on the door, it was opened by Jim's seventeen-year-old daughter, Betsy. She and Andrew sat down in the parlor to talk and immediately liked each other. Betsy's mother invited him to stay for lunch.

Afterward, Andrew asked Betsy to show him around Cushing. To test his character, Betsy had him drive to a place she called Olson's. The old salt-water farm house belonged to a middle-aged brother and sister, Alvaro and Christina Olson. Christina had been crippled by a polio-like illness. Betsy had become friends with Christina and often went over to help her with household chores and to comb her long hair.

Betsy took Andrew to the Olsons' front door. "I wanted to see if he would go in," she said. "A lot of people wouldn't." Inside, the place was grimy, dirty, and smelly, but Andrew was fascinated by the house. He grabbed his drawing pad, sat on the hood of the car, and did a watercolor. Then he marched into the kitchen to meet Christina. He was charmed. "She's just like blueberries to me," he said later. "The Olsons and Christina really were, to me, symbols of New England, Maine, and ancient Maine."

Unable to walk, Christina refused to use crutches or a wheelchair. She stationed herself on a kitchen chair and hitched it across the floor between the table and stove to do the cooking. At night she slept on blankets on the floor of the area that had been the dining room.

Christina and her environment were to become beloved subjects for Andrew. *Christina's World*, his most famous painting, shows her lying in the field below her house. It was inspired by a scene he observed a few years later. He was looking out the window when he saw Christina dragging herself across the grass. The image moved him and later that evening he rushed to his studio and sketched the composition from memory. He did the tempera painting upstairs at the Olsons'. It took months to complete. He began with the house, then the hill, and added Christina last using a drawing of Betsy's body to work out the pose. "I felt the loneliness of that figure," he said, "perhaps the same that I felt myself as a kid."

As they talked that first afternoon, Andrew and Betsy discovered they had both been loners as children. He asked her to go dancing the following week. But the very next day he unexpectedly returned to her house in his father's motorboat, and took Betsy and her sister Gwen to meet his family. N.C. met them on the dock and gave a glare of disapproval at the girls' bathing suits, red lipstick, and nail polish. "I instantly disliked him," said Betsy.

Andrew hustled the girls off to his studio. Gwen, an art major, gushed over Andrew's watercolors. Betsy said nothing. In a corner she noticed his tempera portrait and said, "I like this the best."

Andrew, new at tempera then, felt encouraged. "Betsy really hit the note," he said. "That meant everything to me."

The next Saturday he took her dancing. That night Andrew proposed and Betsy accepted. "And it happened. Just like that," she said. "Boom!"

ANDREW WYETH, *CHRISTINA'S WORLD*, 1948, TEMPERA ON PANEL

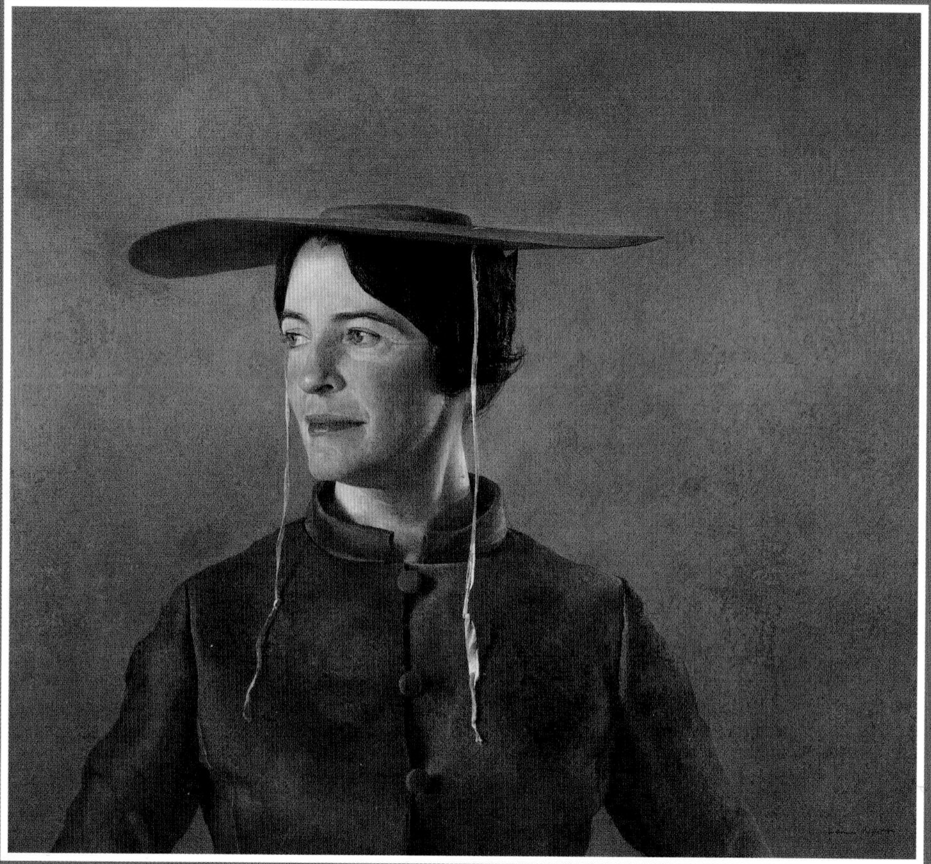

ANDREW WYETH, *MAGA'S DAUGHTER*, 1966, TEMPERA ON PANEL

But they kept their engagement a secret. In September Betsy entered Colby Junior College in New Hampshire. Andrew wrote, "My darling one, . . . I want you to know that I think you are the most beautiful person I've ever known."

Years later he was to capture her beauty in a tempera painting, *Maga's Daughter*, showing Betsy in a Quaker riding hat. Earlier, at the time they were secretly engaged, she came down to Chadds Ford to visit him, and they fell more deeply in love.

That October Andrew had his second show at the Macbeth Gallery. Again nearly all the pictures were bought before the show even opened.

In December N.C.'s painting *Island Funeral* was exhibited at Macbeth's. He had finally achieved his goal and was thrilled with what he termed "my first appearance in N.Y. [New York] as a painter of something other than illustrations." The whole family gathered for the opening. Andrew was late because, without the family's knowledge, he was buying a ring for Betsy.

When they announced their engagement, N.C. worried that marriage would interfere with Andrew's career and offered to build him a studio and support him if he would wait. Andrew refused.

On May 15, 1940, Andrew and Betsy were married. For their honeymoon they spent a few days alone in Port Clyde. Then Andrew went back to painting. "So soon?" asked Betsy.

Andrew replied, "Everything else is going to be secondary."

ONE SUMMER
IN MAINE

Andrew and Betsy settled in the schoolhouse at the edge of N.C.'s property. N.C. visited them daily. He delivered their mail and brought them *The New York Times*. Then he'd go into the studio with Andrew to discuss Andrew's latest painting.

During the day, Betsy wandered in and out of the studio as well, watching Andrew's work in progress. More and more, Andrew trusted Betsy's judgment rather than his father's. She encouraged his tempera painting even though the Macbeth Gallery wasn't interested. For Andrew tempera came closer to conveying the natural colors of the earth. "I wanted something that expresses the country," he said.

On long walks together, Betsy often asked questions about his work. "Why do you see so many colors? Why do you paint the sky lavender when I see it's blue?" Later Andrew said of Betsy, "She's made me into a painter that I would not have been otherwise . . . I had a severe training with my father, but I had a more severe training with Betsy."

Betsy had always loved picking berries, and Andrew wanted to paint a picture of her doing it. But all his drawings seemed ordinary. One summer in Maine he decided to try to capture the scene unobserved. "I sneaked along the edge of the woods and found her sleeping," he said. "I made a

ANDREW WYETH, *DISTANT THUNDER*, 1961, TEMPERA ON PANEL

quick drawing. As I finished it, I could hear thunder way off . . . Suddenly, out of the grass, popped our dog Rattler's head, his ears up, cupped, hearing those distant sounds." Andrew portrayed that moment just *after* Betsy had picked blueberries in the painting titled *Distant Thunder*. But he thought there was too much of her face. So he painted in a hat. "That made the picture," he said.

Daily walks were part of Andrew's painting process. Once, after a hike along the ridge in Chadds Ford, he wrote to his father, "The crows and other birds seemed to be blowing instead of flying through the air, everything was moving. Some day to put this in painting is what I hope to do."

Andrew started a painting from a bird's-eye view of his favorite route. The picture, *Soaring*, features three turkey buzzards flying high above the hills Andrew covered on foot. When the picture was still unfinished, N.C. came into the studio and said, "Andy, that doesn't work. That's not a painting."

Discouraged, Andrew put the picture away. A few years later when the Macbeth Gallery was planning a show of his work, the critic Lincoln Kirstein saw the painting and insisted that Andrew complete it. *Soaring* sold immediately and today hangs in the Shelburne Museum in Vermont.

Andrew's painting career nearly came to an end in December 1941, when the United States entered World War II. All of the Wyeths worried that he would be drafted in the army. N.C. tried to use his influence with important people in Washington, D.C., to keep Andrew out of the war. Andrew's older brother Nat offered to take his place in the draft. But Andrew secretly wanted to join the army. So he registered with the draft board. When he was finally called up for a physical in 1943, he was offered the rank of sergeant as an

ANDREW WYETH, *SOARING*, 1950, TEMPERA ON PANEL

army artist. Just as he was about to ship out to the Solomon Islands, he was rejected because of an arthritic hip condition that he had had since childhood.

Meanwhile, Nat, an engineer with the DuPont Company, had a wartime job considered vitally important. He had invented machinery that produced detonators for antiaircraft guns, and he supervised three thousand defense workers at an explosives plant in New Jersey that operated twenty-four hours a day.

Nat was married to Caroline Pyle, a niece of N.C.'s former teacher, and they had a son, Newell Convers Wyeth II. N.C. adored his little grandson and namesake. When Newell was about a year old, he visited N.C.'s studio and saw the painting of *Jack the Giant-Killer*, an illustration for the *Anthology of Children's Literature*. On his next visit Newell asked for the picture by name. From then on whenever he came to his grandpa's studio he asked, "Can I see the Giant?"

At about the same time, Betsy became pregnant and in 1943 gave birth to Nicholas Wyeth. She and Andrew named the baby for his ancestor who had come from England to Massachusetts in 1645. Unlike his own father, Andrew spent little time taking care of the baby. He was too busy painting. "You've got to be selfish to paint," he said. "I'm much more selfish than my father."

In 1944 Caroline and Nat had a second baby boy and named him Howard Pyle Wyeth. Homesick for family, they moved back to Chadds Ford and rented a farmhouse next to Andrew and Betsy's schoolhouse. Each morning N.C. stopped at the farmhouse and picked up his young grandson Newell and took him driving in his Ford station wagon.

On the morning of October 19, 1945, N.C. set out to pick up a woman who was going to clean the schoolhouse. He took his grandson Newell along with him. As they approached the railroad crossing, N.C. stopped the station wagon and took Newell over to the cornfield to watch a farmer and his wife bundling dried corn shocks. The couple overheard N.C. say to his grandson, "Newell, you won't see this again. Remember this." Then N.C. and Newell got back into the car and headed toward the crossing. The car stalled on the tracks. A locomotive roared toward them. The engineer slammed on the brakes and blew the whistle. But it was too late. The train crashed into the station wagon. N.C. and Newell were killed. N.C. was sixty-two; Newell was three.

The news spread through the Brandywine Valley. Andrew and Betsy were at the farm in Maine and had no telephone. A neighbor drove over and told Andrew to call home. He went to the neighbor's house and spoke to his sister Ann, who told him what had happened. Betsy said he stood there silently, as though he were seeing a ghost. The next morning when she woke up Andrew was standing at the window, sobbing. "By God," he later said, "it took a locomotive to kill N.C. Wyeth."

Andrew grieved over the loss of his father. "I don't think a father and son could have had a warmer relationship," he said. "I loved the things he loved." Painting now became difficult for him. He no longer felt he had an emotional reason to paint. He was furious with himself for never having painted a portrait of his father in life.

A month after the funeral Andrew was struggling with a watercolor near the site of the accident. All of a sudden a boy wearing an old army

jacket and a leather pilot's hat came running down the hill. That image instantly captured Andrew's grief over the death of his father. "The boy was me at a loss," he said. "His hand, drifting in the air, was my hand, groping, my free soul." Andrew quickly made a sketch; then over the course of the entire winter, he worked on a tempera painting of the image. "The hill," he said, "seemed to be breathing—rising and falling—almost as though it was my father's chest." He called the painting *Winter, 1946*.

"I had this terrific urge," said Andrew, "to prove that what my father had started in me was not in vain."

DANGEROUS AND
LOOMING

After N.C.'s death, Andrew said of his childhood home, "The place was like a big ship without a rudder."

His mother stayed in the Big House with Andrew's sister Carolyn. Carolyn had been briefly married but had moved back home and had a studio in part of N.C.'s studio. Andrew often stopped in at the end of the day to visit his mother and sister. He still felt N.C.'s presence all around him. Whenever he finished a painting he wondered, "What would Pa have said?"

At the time of N.C.'s death, Betsy was pregnant. On July 6, 1946, she gave birth to a second son. She and Andrew named him James Browning, but they called the baby Jamie.

Sometimes Andrew took his sons, Nicky and Jamie, along with him when he painted. Often he wound up painting pictures of the boys. One time Jamie dropped a toy soldier in the field, and Andrew went searching for it. When Andrew returned, he found Jamie sitting and daydreaming, his arms clasped around his knees. *Faraway* is a portrait of Jamie, age six, wearing his favorite Davy Crockett coonskin hat and metal-tipped Civil War shoes. Andrew did the painting in drybrush, a technique in which watercolor is applied with a brush squeezed almost completely dry.

ANDREW WYETH, *FARAWAY*, 1952, DRYBRUSH WATERCOLOR ON PAPER

In the years following N.C.'s death, Andrew's work grew more somber. *Wind from the Sea* captures a moment when Andrew was upstairs at the Olsons' house on a hot, humid day. A breeze lifted the curtains. The delicate birds in the pattern of lace symbolized Christina's beauty hidden beneath her deformed body. He said, "Ever since I was a small boy the movement of a curtain in the breeze has thrilled me in a very strange way."

In 1948 Andrew completed *Christina's World,* and it was purchased by the prestigious Museum of Modern Art (MoMA) in New York City. Andrew's fame soared as museums and collectors acquired his work. "I came along at the right moment in American art," he said. The trend at that time was toward abstraction. Energetic new artists celebrated color, shapes, and lines rather than representing recognizable images. Andrew, however, pursued realism, and people responded to his paintings.

In 1950, at age thirty-three, he was elected a member of the National Institute of Arts and Letters. When he showed the letter of invitation to his sister Ann, he burst into tears and said, "Gosh, I wish Pa was alive."

In 1955 Andrew was inducted into the American Academy of Arts and Letters. At age thirty-eight he was the youngest candidate ever chosen. Edward Hopper, an American realist painter he had always admired, was inducted at the same time. At the ceremonies the new members received huge medals draped around their necks like Olympic athletes. After receiving their medals, Andrew whispered to Hopper, "How do you feel?" Hopper replied, "Like a track star."

Collectors clamored for Andrew's work. Sometimes they wanted to buy a painting *before* he had even painted it. In 1956 Joseph Hirshhorn established the Hirshhorn Museum in Washington, D.C., and wrote to Andrew and asked to buy the next picture Andrew made. Prices of Andrew's paintings doubled and redoubled. Andrew said, "It's quite a way to make a living, painting what you like."

But really, money didn't matter to Andrew. It merely allowed him the opportunity to paint. It gave him, he said, "the absolute freedom to do something in the future better than what I've done in the past." Despite his growing fame, Andrew's work habits remained unchanged. He got up

ANDREW WYETH, *WIND FROM THE SEA*, 1947, TEMPERA ON PANEL

every morning at 6:30, left the house at 8, returned at around 6 in the evening, and went to bed at 9:30. Betsy said, "Andy's limited strength is totally burned up each day painting what he feels he must paint."

In 1951 Andrew had developed a disease of his bronchial tubes. Surgeons removed one lobe from his lungs. During the eight-hour operation, Andrew had a near-death experience. He saw Albrecht Dürer, the Renaissance artist whose work he had been studying, beckoning him. Later, Andrew learned that his heart had stopped in the operating room.

After the operation, he took walks in the fields near his home to regain his strength. He wore thigh-high French cavalier boots, a Christmas gift from Betsy. The boots had belonged to N.C.'s teacher, Howard Pyle, and both Pyle and N.C. had used them in illustrations. Andrew worried that he might lose his painting arm because his right shoulder muscles had been cut during the surgery. But soon he was at work on a tempera painting, holding the panel on his lap, with his arm supported in a sling suspended from the ceiling. "To hell with the arm," said Andrew, "I wanted to paint this picture."

The picture, *Trodden Weed*, shows his tall boots stepping through the field, crushing a weed. He said that the black line of the weed represented "the presence of death" that he experienced during his operation. "This painting is highly emotional—dangerous and looming," said Andrew. "I like it."

ANDREW WYETH, *TRODDEN WEED,* **1951, TEMPERA ON PANEL**

GHOST OF N.C. WYETH

Andrew's son Jamie also loved to draw. From the start Jamie showed remarkable talent. "I think it must be in the genes," he once said. His first drawing at age two was of a pumpkin. During his childhood he produced one thousand drawings, which his mother, Betsy, carefully saved.

Jamie liked to play alone in N.C.'s studio up on the hill as his father, Andrew, had done. The studio had been left untouched. N.C.'s birch-bark canoe hung from the ceiling, and the chests were crammed with costumes and props. "It was magical for a child," said Jamie. Sometimes he almost believed that he had known his grandfather.

Also like Andrew before him, Jamie enjoyed dressing up in costumes from N.C.'s collection, and he too liked playing with toy soldiers. Jamie pored over his grandfather's pictures in the books he had illustrated, and he studied Howard Pyle's art with fascination. Inspired, he did his own pen-and-ink drawings illustrating stories his mother read aloud to him. Years later as an adult, Jamie illustrated *The Stray*, a book his mother had written. The children's novel is based on people in Chadds Ford. Jamie, however, portrayed the main character as a dog. Animals, especially dogs, were to become one of his favorite subjects to paint.

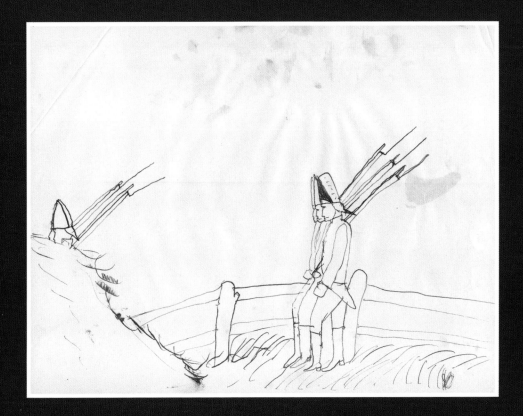

JAMIE WYETH, AN EARLY CHILDHOOD DRAWING OF SOLDIERS,
1951, PEN AND INK ON PAPER

As a boy, Jamie was surrounded by art: his father's paintings at home in the schoolhouse and his aunt Carolyn's pictures in the Big House and in her studio. "It would have been very abnormal for me to be in a room that did not have paint lying around," said Jamie. He liked to wander into N.C.'s studio and observe his aunt Carolyn working. Carolyn, like her father, used oils. "I used to sit and watch Carolyn squirt out the paint," said Jamie, "and it was so luscious the way it poured out."

At age twelve Jamie tried tempera in a painting titled *Merlin,* but he left it unfinished. "You have to love a medium to work in it," he said. "I love the feel and smell of oil."

Jamie's older brother, Nicky, showed no interest in drawing or painting. Much like his uncle Nat, Nicky liked to build things. He made kites and model airplanes, which he hung from the ceiling in his room. Nicky had inherited a malformation of his hips from his father. Because of his frequent absences, Nicky was miserable at school. Finally, in the sixth grade, he asked to go to boarding school in New Hampshire. Andrew and Betsy hated the separation from their son but they wanted to do what was best for him.

Meanwhile, at home, Jamie thought about what he would do when he grew up. He considered becoming an airplane pilot. Then he decided to become a butler and practiced by serving dinner to his parents.

But by the age of twelve, Jamie knew he wanted to become an artist. "All I wanted to do was draw and paint," he said. So despite his mother's protests, he dropped out of sixth grade and was home tutored as his father had been. After tutoring sessions in the morning, Jamie studied art in the afternoon with his aunt Carolyn right in N.C.'s studio.

JAMIE WYETH, ILLUSTRATION FROM *THE STRAY*, 1979, PEN AND INK ON PAPER

Carolyn followed her father's traditional teaching methods and even wore his long brown coat. She had many students, and Jamie drew in charcoal along with the others. "It wasn't interesting, but it was important," he said. "It was a lot of drawing cubes and shapes and just working in black and white," said Jamie. "No painting ... which I think probably was good. I think it was to instill some discipline—if I was going to paint I really better buckle down."

After two years of apprenticeship with his aunt, Jamie, at age fourteen, began painting in oils on his own. Although his father never formally taught him, Jamie regarded Andrew as "the greatest teacher." Unlike his own father, N.C., Andrew would never touch up Jamie's painting, or tell him that he had used the wrong color. But when Jamie worked on a portrait, Andrew would make a comment. "Jamie, be aware of its [the ear's] relationship to the head, to the nose, to the eye," he would say. And every year Jamie and Andrew would sit on the floor together and paint dozens of Christmas cards.

In summing up his art training Jamie said, "I had the ghost of N.C. Wyeth, who was this magical being ... His knights in armor excited me much more than what my father was working on. But my father was working constantly, from the minute the sun came up ... a role model for total absorption—the belief that painting is a serious business."

JAMIE WYETH, HAND PAINTED CHRISTMAS CARDS,
LEFT: *WREATH CATCHING HAT*, 1957, PEN AND INK ON PAPER
RIGHT: *CHRISTMAS HORN*, 1956, PEN AND INK ON PAPER

PORTRAITS

Jamie's parents purchased a group of eighteenth-century mill buildings a mile up the Brandywine River from Chadds Ford. Betsy, who had always been interested in architecture and design, began to restore the buildings as living quarters. "I love things that need attention," she said.

In 1961, when the granary was completed, Andrew, Betsy, and Jamie moved in. Although Betsy had planned a new studio for Andrew, he preferred painting in his studio at the schoolhouse. Andrew hated change. Jamie took the adjoining room in the schoolhouse as his studio, but Andrew annoyed him by playing classical music while he worked. Two years later Betsy finished restoration of the mill, and she and Andrew moved in there. Jamie then stayed on at the granary on his own.

Andrew portrayed the gristmill in his painting *Night Sleeper*, which shows his dog Nel asleep. "I woke up one night and went downstairs," said Andrew, "and there was my dog Nel with this strange expression on her face." He made a drawing and a watercolor of her head. But the image kept bubbling in his mind, and he made drawings of the mill in moonlight. At last he began painting in tempera on a panel six feet long. He called the painting *Night Sleeper* because, said Andrew, "that patch of light [on the

ANDREW WYETH, *NIGHT SLEEPER*, 1979, TEMPERA ON PANEL

bag and on the window frame] reminded me of the sleeper trains I used to take to Maine when I was a child."

Andrew's dog paintings fascinated Jamie. He had started doing his own at age eight or nine when he drew pictures of Eloise, the family's poodle. "The thing about dogs is that they have continued to interest me through my whole career," said Jamie. "When I choose to paint a dog, usually it's a dog I've known and lived with."

Jamie has done many paintings of the dogs he has owned over the years. Kleberg, a hunting dog, liked to sit next to Jamie's easel while he worked. One day, for fun, Jamie painted a black circle around Kleberg's eye. "He loved it, and I loved it," said Jamie, so Jamie "freshened" the circle about once a month with mustache dye. And people marveled at the dog's unusual markings.

JAMIE WYETH, *WOOLWORTH POODLE DRAWING*, 1958, PENCIL ON PAPER

JAMIE WYETH, *KLEBERG STUDY—WHITE WASH*, 1984, COMBINED MEDIUMS ON TONED BOARD

Jamie paints with what he calls "combined mediums." He said, "In my studio, I have pastels lying on the floor, I have watercolor, oil, charcoal, and I like jumping back and forth. I use my fingers mostly and sticks and pieces of cloth. I use brushes less and less."

By the time he was eighteen, Jamie's work hung in the Farnsworth Art Museum and the Wilmington Society of Art. When Jamie was nineteen, he went to New York City and lived there for a few months. Every Saturday he worked at a morgue to study anatomy and learn more about human form. He put this knowledge to use in his portraits and figure paintings.

In 1966 Jamie joined the U.S. Air Corps Reserve and went to Amarillo, Texas, for basic training. Even while in the military, he used his artistic skills. One of his assignments during his four years of service was to create an enormous mural, twenty-three feet long, for a battalion ball. He did the painting on parachute silk and used trash-can covers as palettes.

Years earlier, before Jamie went into the service, he had met a girl named Phyllis Mills. A year after they first met, Phyllis broke her neck in an automobile accident and was paralyzed from the waist down. Gradually she learned how to walk with crutches and braces, encouraged by her friend John F. Kennedy. She worked for Kennedy when he was a senator, and then when he was president. Later, when Jamie was twenty-one, he spotted Phyllis again at a horse race in Pennsylvania. Fascinated by her, he watched her from a distance through his binoculars. Jamie renewed their acquaintance and asked her to pose.

Phyllis introduced Jamie to the Kennedy clan. In 1967 Jackie Kennedy, the president's widow, asked Jamie to do a portrait of the president. Jamie

had never met President John F. Kennedy or even seen him in a public appearance. President Kennedy had been assassinated in 1963, when Jamie was just seventeen years old. Jamie's father discouraged him from accepting the commission. He didn't believe that an artist could do a good portrait from photographs. But Jamie took the job. He was twenty years old.

Jamie spent weeks watching Kennedy family movies and archival films. He talked with Jackie and sketched the president's brothers, Bobby and Ted, to capture a family resemblance. Finally he completed *Portrait of John F. Kennedy*. The painting shows the President with a thoughtful expression, as though he is contemplating a difficult problem. Bobby disliked the painting and felt it was inappropriate for the White House. Jackie, however, loved it.

JAMIE WYETH, *PORTRAIT OF JOHN F. KENNEDY*, 1967, OIL ON CANVAS

While Jamie worked on the portrait, he and Phyllis grew closer. They were married in 1968. Since then they have lived on a working farm in Delaware, just across the way from Chadds Ford.

Jamie has painted many portraits of Phyllis. *And Then into the Deep Gorge* shows her driving a cart pulled by two of her beloved horses.

At age twenty-three he painted *Portrait of Andrew Wyeth*, a serious and moving image. Jamie said, "When I work on a portrait, it's really osmosis. I try to become the person I'm painting."

Jamie began doing large-scale portraits of animals. "I only paint animals I have known," he said. "I get as involved with a sheep as I do with a president of the United States."

JAMIE WYETH, *PORTRAIT OF ANDREW WYETH*, 1969, OIL ON CANVAS

One of Jamie's most popular paintings features Den Den, a six-hundred-pound pig. Jamie met Den Den at a nearby farm where he had gone to paint. "Den Den had the run of the place," said Jamie. "I was walking when I heard this snorting." Jamie stuck his head around the corner and saw cerulean blue on the pig's snout. "She had eaten twenty-two tubes of oil paint!" Jamie had heard that oil paint was toxic for animals because of the lead content, and he worried that the pig would die. She survived, but the farmer planned to butcher her. Jamie said to the farmer, "I'm taking her," and he kept Den Den as a pet.

The pig would come when Jamie called her and would lie down when he scratched her belly. Jamie brought Den Den into his house and posed her in front of the fireplace. "When you get eye-to-eye contact with an animal, a real connection, it's limitless," he said. His *Portrait of Pig*, five feet by seven feet, is almost life-size. It was a hit at the opening of the Brandywine River Museum in 1971. The vigorous strokes made with sticks or brush handles convey the texture of the pig's bristles and the coarse hay at her feet. Warm tones of pink and gold tenderly suggest her great bulk. He wanted the picture to be truthful. "Pigs are *not* cute," he said. "They do eat their young. This one happened to be a friend of mine."

Den Den lived to be nineteen, an old age for a pig. But she became immortal through Jamie's portrait.

JAMIE WYETH, *PORTRAIT OF PIG*, 1970, OIL ON CANVAS

WOLF DOG

Jamie has said, "Painting is agonizing but addictive. There are moments when it is inspiring, but they are few and far between." With each new painting he asked himself, "Will it stack up to *Christina's World*?" his father's most famous work.

Reviewers frequently attacked Jamie's paintings as too traditional, too "illustrative," too much in the Wyeth tradition. Jamie said that being a Wyeth made it hard for people to see his work "clearly and deeply. I'm just a name," he said. After a while Jamie was half relieved when reviewers ignored his shows.

In the late 1970s he became pals with Pop artist Andy Warhol. "Warhol fascinated me," said Jamie. "He had a wonderful sense of wonder, very childlike."

In 1976 Jamie and Warhol decided to do portraits of each other. Jamie began with studies of Andy holding Archie, one of his precious dachshunds. "Archie was always with him," recalled Jamie. "They had the same stare." On the opening night of their portrait exhibit at the Coe Kerr Gallery, police had to hold back the crowds with barricades.

Like his father and grandfather, Jamie divided his time between the countryside along the Brandywine River and the coast of Maine. When he

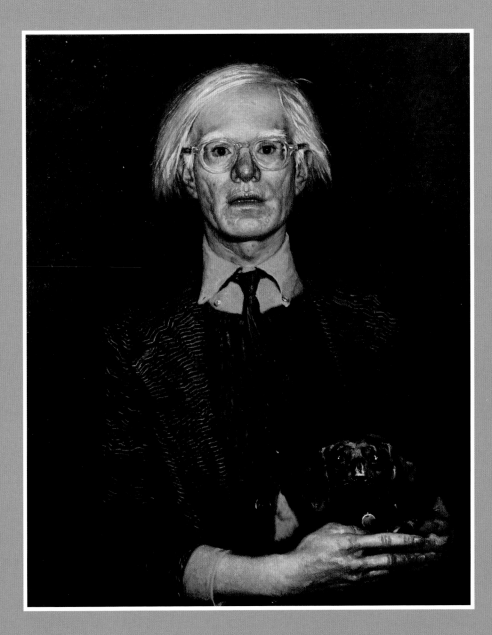

JAMIE WYETH, *PORTRAIT OF ANDY WARHOL*, 1976, OIL ON PANEL

was fifteen, he made his first solo sail to Monhegan Island, fifteen miles from his home. The island's wild and rocky setting had long been a prized destination for artists such as Edward Hopper and Rockwell Kent. Kent, best known for his woodblock engravings and pen-and-ink drawings, had illustrated *Moby Dick*, one of Jamie's favorite books. Jamie fell in love with the island too, and in 1967 he bought artist Rockwell Kent's house.

On Monhegan and the nearby islands, Jamie painted pictures of houses, geese, sheep, pounding waves, and seagulls wheeling above. One of his paintings is a portrait, *Wolf Dog*. Jamie had been to Alaska and had met mushers, who drive dogs that pull sleds. "This guy offered to send me a lead dog," said Jamie. "The dog was shipped to the island, and it was three-quarters wolf and one-quarter malamute." The musher sent instructions: "Do not take him [the

JAMIE WYETH, *WOLF DOG*, 1976, OIL ON CANVAS

wolf dog] into your house, do not treat him as a pet, leave him outside."

The wolf dog, named George, howled all night the first week Jamie had him. Neighbors on the island complained. So Jamie brought George into the house. "He [George] had these pure white eyes which were really scary," said Jamie. "At night he ended up in my room. I would wake up and feel someone staring at me, and he would be standing next to my bed, staring. After I finished the painting I sent him back to Alaska. I didn't keep him because he would instantly kill anything smaller than himself."

Jamie also used friends and neighbors as models. He featured Cat Bates, a local boy from Monhegan Island, in his painting titled *Inferno, Monhegan*. The painting shows Cat burning trash in an incinerator, and in the background there is a lobster boat moored in Monhegan harbor.

JAMIE WYETH, *INFERNO, MONHEGAN*, 2006, COMBINED MEDIUMS ON CORRUGATED BOARD

JAMIE WYETH, *KALOUNNA IN FROG TOWN*, 1986, OIL ON PANEL

At his other home in Delaware, Jamie did studies of an eleven-year-old boy named Kalounna. Kalounna's family were refugees from Laos, and they worked as caretakers on Jamie and Phyllis's farm. Every day after school, from 3:30 to 5:30 P.M., Kalounna posed for Jamie. It was the boy's first paying job. As the setting for the portrait *Kalounna in Frog Town*, Jamie chose a small community near Chadds Ford. He composed the picture with Kalounna, wearing a red T-shirt, in the center. In the background there is a farmhouse with red shutters and a red trailer-truck. When Jamie asked the owner of the trailer-truck permission to paint it, the owner misunderstood and said, "But I like the color as it is."

In the meantime, Jamie's father, Andrew, had turned to painting female figures, a classical subject in art. "You don't want to sit down and do the same thing you've done for the past thirty years," said Andrew. "That's boring."

Starting in 1972, Andrew began a series of paintings of Helga Testorf, a Prussian nurse who took care of his sister Carolyn, who was partly crippled due to a fall years earlier. Carolyn still lived in the Big House with her mother, Carol, and she ran an art school in N.C.'s studio and painted in a smaller studio.

In 1973 Carol died and willed the house to all the children. It was decided that Carolyn would stay there for the rest of her life. Carolyn had become more eccentric. She had strange shopping sprees and bought hundreds of tubes of oil paint and forty pairs of tweezers. She fed her dogs steak and lobster and didn't care when they relieved themselves on the antique Persian rugs. The other Wyeth siblings were disgusted, but Andrew said of Carolyn, "She could never shock me, and I could never shock her. We did what we damned pleased."

Because Andrew wanted to keep the Helga-inspired work a secret, Carolyn turned her studio over to him. Over the next fifteen years, he produced temperas, dry brushes, watercolors, and pencil studies of Helga such as the painting *Braids*. No one knows exactly how many images he made, although it has been estimated as two hundred and forty. During that period he also did many temperas on other subjects, including *Night Sleeper*.

Jamie and Nicky were the only family members who knew about the Helga project, but they kept silent. When Andrew showed Jamie a few watercolors of Helga, Jamie recognized that it was "important work."

In 1985 Andrew finally showed the Helga paintings to Betsy. When she first beheld them in the gallery of their gristmill, she said, "*Whew!* I was absolutely overcome."

The Helga collection was exhibited at the National Gallery of Art in Washington, D.C. From there, the art went on a national tour and then traveled to Japan. The show sparked tremendous interest and curiosity. But critics objected to the popularity of the show. Andrew said to his sister Carolyn, "I don't think anyone ever had worse reviews. What's it matter? I'm a grown-up. I believe in myself."

"I may never paint again," he told people. After that, Andrew began a series of temperas and watercolors, experimenting with new techniques. He said, "You want to improve, and you do *know* more. So you think things will get a little easier. But it gets harder with age."

ANDREW WYETH, *BRAIDS*, 1979, TEMPERA ON PANEL

ILLUSTRATING MY LIFE

In the years following the Helga uproar, Andrew and Betsy quietly resumed their routine, spending winters in Chadds Ford and summers in Maine. Betsy had bought three small islands in Maine and designed and built houses on them. In 1990 she and Andrew gave Southern Island to Jamie, where he moved to have more privacy. He continues to live in a lighthouse there, going back and forth between that island and the Delaware farm and Monhegan Island.

Jamie continued to be fascinated by island life and painted pictures of ravens, seagulls, goats, coon cats, and even a goose. Even when he was painting these subjects, his dogs kept him company. And he did sketches and portraits of them—Ziggy, Tiller, Theo, Wiley, and Homer (named for the artist Winslow Homer). In the winter of 2005, Jamie went to the White House to sketch President George W. Bush's Scotch terriers, Barney and Miss Beazley Bush, and his cat, India, frolicking on the snowy lawn.

"I work all day every day," said Jamie. "I have no hobbies. I paint all the time. Most of it winds up in the wastebasket." Like his father, he keeps a sketchpad next to his bed.

Frequently Jamie is asked to illustrate children's books, bringing the Wyeth legacy full circle. Jamie said, "We're charged, my father and I, with being a pack of illustrators. I've always taken it as a supreme compliment. What's wrong with illustration?"

THE WHITE HOUSE
WASHINGTON

JAMIE WYETH, *MISS BEAZLEY AND BARNEY CONFERRING, INDIA TAKING NOTES*
(WHITE HOUSE STATIONERY), 2005, PENCIL AND INK ON PAPER

The question of whether illustration is as great an art as fine art has been debated by artists and critics for centuries. But Andrew didn't feel there was any difference. He once said, "I was really illustrating my life when I began to paint."

When Jamie illustrates a book, the storytelling process inspires his art as it did his grandfather's. "I'm sent a lot of manuscripts," said Jamie, but he turns down most of them. In 1997, however, he illustrated *Cabbages and Kings*, a story about an asparagus trying to grow and survive in a vegetable garden. Most recently Jamie did paintings in combined media for *Sammy in the Sky*. "The story struck me as moving, a special story."

The picture book tells about the death of a girl's beloved pet, her dog Sammy, and how she copes with her loss by sharing happy memories of him. As the model for Sammy, Jamie used a "combination of dogs," various dogs that he had known.

On January 16, 2009, Jamie's father, Andrew Wyeth, died in his sleep in Chadds Ford. He was ninety-one. One of his very last paintings, done in 2008, is a watercolor of a motorcyclist at a red traffic light and is titled *Stop*. In obituaries he was hailed as one of the most popular artists in the history of American art. His work had raised questions about the theory of art. Was it wrong for an artist to be popular? Were Andrew's realistic paintings that appealed to such a wide audience simply old-fashioned? Jamie said of his father while he was still alive, "I happen to think that Andrew Wyeth is certainly the greatest living painter, and that is tough to live up to—but it is also a great goal."

In an interview with *Time* magazine, Andrew had discussed his goal. He said, "I want to show Americans what America is like."

JAMIE WYETH, "ALBERT SQUEEZED HIS EYES SHUT AS THE DOG RAN PAST"
FROM *CABBAGES AND KINGS*, 1996, COMBINED MEDIUMS ON PAPER

He did, in wintry landscapes of rural Pennsylvania, and summer scenes of Maine painted in loving detail. And so did his father, N.C. Wyeth, as he portrayed George Washington in the Battle of the Brandywine and cowboys roping cattle out West. Today Jamie Wyeth carries on the tradition with vibrant portraits that range from pigs on a Delaware farm to presidential dogs romping at the White House.

Jamie, Andrew, and N.C. Wyeth, three generations of artists.

N.C. WYETH   ANDREW WYETH   JAMIE WYETH

Artwork Locations

Many of the works of N.C., Andrew, and Jamie Wyeth are held in private collections. The following are available for public viewing.

N.C. WYETH

p. 9 *JIM HAWKINS LEAVES HOME* (from *Treasure Island*), 1911, oil on canvas. Brandywine River Museum, Chadds Ford, Pennsylvania.

p. 13 *CUTTING OUT (COLORADO)*, 1904, oil on canvas. Buffalo Bill Historical Center, Cody, Wyoming.

p. 25 *THE SIEGE OF THE ROUND-HOUSE* (from *Kidnapped*), 1913, oil on canvas. Brandywine River Museum, Chadds Ford, Pennsylvania.

p. 27 *ROBIN MEETS MAID MARIAN* (from *Robin Hood*), 1917, oil on canvas. New York Public Library, New York.

p. 34 *IN A DREAM I MEET GENERAL WASHINGTON*, 1930–31, oil on canvas. Brandywine River Museum, Chadds Ford, Pennsylvania.

p. 52 *ISLAND FUNERAL*, 1939, tempera on panel. The Hotel DuPont Collection of American Art, Wilmington, Delaware.

ANDREW WYETH

p. 49 *THE LOBSTERMAN*, 1937, watercolor on paper. Hunter Museum of Art, Chattanooga, Tennessee.

p. 51 *THE REVENANT*, 1949, tempera on panel. The New Britain Museum of American Art, New Britain, Connecticut.

p. 55 *CHRISTINA'S WORLD*, 1948, tempera on panel. Museum of Modern Art, New York.

p. 61 *SOARING*, 1950, tempera on panel. Shelburne Museum, Shelburne, Vermont.

p. 64 *WINTER, 1946*, 1946, tempera on panel. North Carolina Museum of Art, Raleigh, North Carolina.

p. 69 *WIND FROM THE SEA*, 1947, tempera on panel. National Gallery of Art, Washington D.C.

JAMIE WYETH

p. 87 *PORTRAIT OF PIG*, 1970, oil on canvas. Brandywine River Museum, Chadds Ford, Pennsylvania.

p. 89 *PORTRAIT OF ANDY WARHOL*, 1976, oil on panel. Cheekwood Botanical Gardens and Museum of Art, Nashville, Tennessee.

p. 92 *KALOUNNA IN FROG TOWN*, 1986, oil on panel. Daniel J. Terra Collection, Terra Museum of American Art, Chicago, Illinois.

Image Credits

Jacket Counterclockwise from top right: Photo of Andrew Wyeth (detail) © 1997 by Victoria Browning Wyeth. Photo of N.C. Wyeth (detail) courtesy of the Wyeth Family Archive. Photo of Jamie Wyeth (detail) © 1997 by Victoria Browning Wyeth. *THEY FOUGHT WITH HIM ON FOOT...* (detail) 1917 by N.C. Wyeth. *FARAWAY* © 1952 Andrew Wyeth. *KLEBERG* (detail) © 1984 Jamie Wyeth.

p. 9 *JIM HAWKINS LEAVES HOME* (from *Treasure Island*), 1911, oil on canvas. Collection Brandywine River Museum, Chadds Ford, Pennsylvania. Acquisition made possible through the generosity of Patricia Wiman Hewitt, 1994.

p. 13 *CUTTING OUT (COLORADO)*, 1904, oil on canvas. Buffalo Bill Historical Center, Cody, Wyoming. Gift of John M. Schiff.

p. 17 N.C. Wyeth on horseback, 1904, photographer unknown. Courtesy of the Wyeth Family Archives.

p. 21 ENDPAPER ILLUSTRATION (from *Treasure Island*), 1911, oil on canvas. Collection Brandywine River Museum, Chadds Ford, Pennsylvania. Purchased in memory of Hope Montgomery Scott, 1997.

p. 25 *THE SIEGE OF THE ROUND-HOUSE* (from *Kidnapped*), 1913, oil on canvas. Collection Brandywine River Museum, Chadds Ford, Pennsylvania. Bequest of Mrs. Russell G. Colt, 1986.

p. 27 *ROBIN MEETS MAID MARIAN* (from *Robin Hood*), 1917, oil on canvas. New York Public Library.

p. 29 *THEY FOUGHT WITH HIM ON FOOT MORE THAN THREE HOURS, BOTH BEFORE HIM AND BEHIND HIM* (from *The Boy's King Arthur*), 1917, oil on canvas. Private collection.

p. 31 *ANDY WITH FIRE ENGINE*, 1923, oil on canvas. Private collection.

p. 34 *IN A DREAM I MEET GENERAL WASHINGTON*, 1930-31, oil on canvas. Collection Brandywine River Museum, Chadds Ford, Pennsylvania. Purchased with funds given in memory of George T. Weymouth, 1991.

p. 37 *PORTRAIT OF ANN READING*, 1930, oil on canvas. The Jamie and Phyllis Wyeth collection.

p. 39 *JACK-BE-NIMBLE*, 1976, watercolor on paper, © Andrew Wyeth. Private collection.

p. 39 *PUMPKINHEAD-SELF-PORTRAIT*, 1972, oil on canvas, © Jamie Wyeth. Private collection.

p. 41 *OLD KRIS*, 1925, oil on canvas. The Wyeth Foundation.

p. 43 *CASTLE SIEGE*, 1932, pen and ink on paper, © Andrew Wyeth. Private collection.

p. 45 Andrew Wyeth at his easel, c. 1935, photographer unknown. Courtesy of the Wyeth Family Archives.

p. 46 N.C. Wyeth posing with his new Cadillac, 1928, photographer unknown. Courtesy of the Wyeth Family Archives.

p. 49 *THE LOBSTERMAN*, 1937, watercolor on paper, © Andrew Wyeth. Hunter Museum of Art, Chattanooga, Tennessee. Gift of the Benwood Foundation.

p. 51 *THE REVENANT*, 1949, tempera on panel, © Andrew Wyeth. The New Britain Museum of American Art, New Britain, Connecticut. Harriet and Russell Stanley Fund.

p. 52 *ISLAND FUNERAL*, 1939, tempera on panel. Hotel DuPont, Wilmington, Delaware.

p. 55 *CHRISTINA'S WORLD*, 1948, tempera on panel, © Andrew Wyeth. Museum of Modern Art, New York.

p. 56 *MAGA'S DAUGHTER*, 1966, tempera on panel, © Andrew Wyeth. Private collection.

p 59 *DISTANT THUNDER*, 1961, tempera on panel, © Andrew Wyeth. Private collection.

p. 61 *SOARING*, 1950, tempera on panel, © Andrew Wyeth. Shelburne Museum, Shelburne, Vermont.

p. 64 *WINTER, 1946*, 1946, tempera on panel, © Andrew Wyeth. North Carolina Museum of Art, Raleigh, North Carolina.

p. 67 *FARAWAY*, 1952, drybrush watercolor on paper, © Andrew Wyeth. The Jamie and Phyllis Wyeth collection.

p. 69 *WIND FROM THE SEA*, 1947, tempera on panel, © Andrew Wyeth. National Gallery of Art, Washington D.C. Gift of Charles H. Morgan.

p. 71 *TRODDEN WEED*, 1951, tempera on panel, © Andrew Wyeth. Private collection.

p. 73 AN EARLY CHILDHOOD DRAWING OF SOLDIERS, 1951, pen and ink on paper, © Jamie Wyeth. The Jamie and Phyllis Wyeth collection.

p. 75 "HE SENT ME OFF TO FIND HIM, BUT IT WAS LYNCH WHO DISCOVERED HIM ON A LIMB OF AN APPLE TREE ENJOYING A MIDMORNING SNACK," (from *The Stray*) 1979, pen and ink on paper, © Jamie Wyeth. The Jamie and Phyllis Wyeth collection.

p. 77 *WREATH CATCHING HAT*, 1957, and *CHRISTMAS HORN*, 1956, pen and ink on paper, © Jamie Wyeth. The Jamie and Phyllis Wyeth collection.

p. 79 *NIGHT SLEEPER*, 1979, tempera on panel, © Andrew Wyeth. Private collection.

p. 80 *WOOLWORTH POODLE DRAWING*, 1958, pencil on paper, © Jamie Wyeth. The Jamie and Phyllis Wyeth collection.

p. 81 *KLEBERG STUDY—WHITE WASH*, 1984, combined mediums on toned board, © Jamie Wyeth. The Jamie and Phyllis Wyeth collection.

p. 83 *PORTRAIT OF JOHN F. KENNEDY*, 1967, oil on canvas, © Jamie Wyeth. The Jamie and Phyllis Wyeth collection.

p. 84 *AND THEN INTO THE DEEP GORGE*, 1975, oil on canvas, © Jamie Wyeth. The Jamie and Phyllis Wyeth collection.

p. 85 *PORTRAIT OF ANDREW WYETH*, 1969, oil on canvas, © Jamie Wyeth. Private collection.

p. 87 *PORTRAIT OF PIG*, 1970, oil on canvas, © Jamie Wyeth. Collection Brandywine River Museum, Chadds Ford, Pennsylvania. Gift of Betsy James Wyeth, 1984.

p. 89 *PORTRAIT OF ANDY WARHOL*, 1976, oil on panel, © Jamie Wyeth. Cheekwood Botanical Gardens and Museum of Art, Nashville, Tennessee.

p. 90 *WOLF DOG*, 1976, oil on canvas, © Jamie Wyeth. Private collection.

p. 91 *INFERNO, MONHEGAN*, 2006, combined mediums on corrugated board, © Jamie Wyeth. Private collection.

p. 92 *KALOUNNA IN FROG TOWN*, 1986, oil on panel, © Jamie Wyeth. Daniel J. Terra Collection, Terra Museum of American Art, Chicago, Illinois.

p. 95 *BRAIDS*, 1979, tempera on panel, © Pacific Sun Trading Company. Courtesy of Frank Fowler and Warren Adelson. Private collection.

p. 97 *MISS BEAZLEY AND BARNEY CONFERRING, INDIA TAKING NOTES*, 2005, pencil and ink on paper, © Jamie Wyeth. The Jamie and Phyllis Wyeth collection.

p. 99 "ALBERT SQUEEZED HIS EYES SHUT AS THE DOG RAN PAST" (from *Cabbages and Kings*), 1996, combined mediums on paper, © Jamie Wyeth. The Jamie and Phyllis Wyeth collection.

p. 100 See Jacket photo credits.

Bibliography

The biography of N.C. Wyeth by David Michaelis, the biography of Andrew Wyeth by Richard Meryman, and Andrew Wyeth's *Autobiography* were especially useful in research. The quotations from these books have appeared in several places in various forms. Because of constrictions of space I have omitted source notes of quotes. However, source notes are available online upon request at www.susangoldmanrubin.com.

BOOKS

Creswick, Paul. *Robin Hood*. Illustrated by N.C. Wyeth. Philadelphia: David McKay, Publisher, 1917.

Duff, James H., Andrew Wyeth, Thomas Hoving, and Lincoln Kirstein. *An American Vision: Three Generations of Wyeth Art*. New York: Bulfinch Press in association with the Brandywine River Museum, 1987.

Lanier, Sidney. *The Boy's King Arthur*. Mineola, New York: Dover Publications, 2006 (unabridged republication of the edition published by Charles Scribner's Sons, New York, in 1917).

Meryman, Richard. *Andrew Wyeth: A Secret Life*. New York: HarperPerennial, 1996.

_____. *Andrew Wyeth: First Impressions*. New York: Harry N. Abrams Inc., 1991.

Michaelis, David. *N.C. Wyeth: A Biography*. New York: Alfred A. Knopf, 1999.

Seabrook, Elizabeth. *Cabbages and Kings*. Paintings by Jamie Wyeth. New York: Viking, a division of Penguin Books USA Inc., 1997.

Stevenson, Robert Louis. *Kidnapped*. Illustrated by N.C. Wyeth. New York: Atheneum Books for Young Readers, 2004. Illustrated edition by N.C. Wyeth originally published 1913 by Charles Scribner's Sons.

_____. *Treasure Island*. New York: Atheneum Books for Young Readers, 1911.

Walsh, Barbara. *Sammy in the Sky*. Paintings by Jamie Wyeth. Somerville: Candlewick Press, 2011.

Wyeth, Andrew. *Autobiography*. Introduction by Thomas Hoving. Old Saybrook, CT: Konecky & Konecky, 1995.

Wyeth, Betsy James. *The Stray*. Drawings by Jamie Wyeth. New York: Farrar Straus Giroux, 1979.

Wyeth, Jamie. *Dog Days*. Chadds Ford: Brandywine River Museum, 2007.

VIDEOS

Andrew Wyeth: Self-Portrait: Snow Hill. Produced by Betsy James Wyeth, directed by Bo Bartlett, and narrated by Stacy Keach. Chip Taylor Communications, 1995.

The Wyeths: A Father and His Family. Produced and directed by David Grubin. The James S. McDonnell Foundation, Smithsonian World, a co-production of WETA, Washington, D.C., and the Smithsonian Institution, 1986.

INTERVIEW WITH AUTHOR ON THE PHONE

Jamie Wyeth, August 27, 2010.

Index

Page numbers in italics indicate photographs.

A

And Then into the Deep Gorge, 84
Andy with Fire Engine, 31
Anthology of Children's Literature, 62

B

Bates, Cat, 91
Bockius, Carol. *See* Wyeth, Carol Bockius
The Boy's King Arthur, 28, *29*
Braids, 94, *95*
Brandywine River Museum, 6, 86
Bronco Buster, 14
Bush, George, W., 96

C

Cabbages and Kings, 98, *99*
Castle Siege, *43*
Chapin, Joseph, 16, 23
Christina's World, 54, *55*, 68
Coe Kerr Gallery, 88
Collier's Weekly, 11
Cutting Out (Colorado), *13*

D

Distant Thunder, *59*, 60
Dürer, Albrecht, 42, 70

F

Faraway, 66, *67*
Farnsworth Art Museum, 6, 82

G

The German, 30

H

Hearst, William Randolph, 26
Hirshhorn, Joseph, 68–69
Hirshhorn Museum, 69
Hopper, Edward, 68, 90
Hurd, Henriette Wyeth, 6, 20, 32, 33, 44, 48
Hurd, Peter, 36, 44, 48

I

In a Dream I Meet General Washington, 33, *34*, 35
Inferno, Monhegan, *91*
Island Funeral, *52*, 53, 57

J

Jack-Be-Nimble, 38, *39*
Jack the Giant-Killer, 62
James, Betsy. *See* Wyeth, Betsy James
James, Merle, 53
Jim Hawkins Leaves Home, *9*

K

Kalounna in Frog Town, *92*, 93
Kennedy, Bobby, 83
Kennedy, Jackie, 82, 83
Kennedy, John F., 82, *83*
Kennedy, Ted, 83
Kent, Rockwell, 90
Kidnapped, 24, *25*
Kleberg Study—White Wash, *81*
Kuerner, Karl and Anna, 30

L

Lawrence, David, 36
The Lobsterman, *49*

M

Macbeth, Robert, 47, 53
Macbeth Gallery, 22, 47, 48, 57, 58, 60
Maga's Daughter, *56*, 57
McCoy, Ann Wyeth, 26, 30, *32*, 35, 36, *37*, 40, 44, 68
McCoy, John, 44
Men of Concord, 46
Merlin, 74
The Merry Adventures of Robin Hood, 11
Mills, Phyllis. *See* Wyeth, Phyllis Mills
Miss Beazley and Barney Conferring, India Taking Notes, 96, *97*
Moby Dick, 90
Moore, Guernsey, 12, 14
Museum of Modern Art (MoMA), 68

N

National Gallery of Art, 94
Night Sleeper, 78, *79*, 94

O

Old Kris, *41*
Olson, Alvaro, 53
Olson, Christina, 53–54, *55*, 68

P

Philadelphia Art Alliance, 47
Portrait of Andrew Wyeth, 84, *85*
Portrait of Andy Warhol, 88, *89*
Portrait of Ann Reading, 35, *37*
Portrait of John F. Kennedy, *83*
Portrait of Pig, 86, *87*
Pumpkinhead-Self-Portrait, 38, *39*
Pyle, Caroline. *See* Wyeth, Caroline Pyle
Pyle, Howard, 11, 12, 14–16, 18, 19, 36, 42, 70, 72

R

The Revenant, 50, *51*
Robin Hood, 26, *27*
Robin Meets Maid Marian, *27*

S

Sammy in the Sky, 98
The Saturday Evening Post, 11, 12, 14, 22
Scribner's, 16, 23, 24
Scribner's Magazine, 11, 16, 18, 19, 22
The Siege of the Round-House, *25*
Soaring, 60, *61*
Stevenson, Robert Louis, 22, 24
Stop, 98
The Stray, 72, *75*

T

Testorf, Helga, 93, 94, *95*
They Fought with Him on Foot More than Three
 Hours, Both Before Him and Behind Him, 28, *29*
Thoreau, Henry David, 22, 28, 46
Treasure Island, *9*, 11, *21*, 22–23, 24
Trodden Weed, 70, *71*

W

Walden, 22
Warhol, Andy, 88, *89*
Wilmington Society of Art, 82
Wind from the Sea, 68, *69*
Winter, 1946, 63, *64*
Wolf Dog, *90*, 91
Woolworth Poodle Drawing, *80*
Wyeth, Andrew. *See also individual artworks*
 awards given to, 68
 birth of, 28
 childhood of, 6, 30, *32*, 33, 35–36, 38, 40
 death of, 98

early art of, 46–48, 50
 family life of, 62, 74
 health problems of, 70
 Jamie's relationship with, 76, 78, 94, 98
 marries Betsy James, 53–54, 57
 N.C.'s relationship with, 35, 42, 44–48, 50, 58,
  60, 63, 66
 photographs of, *32*, *45*, *100*
 portraits of, 30, *31*, 84, *85*
Wyeth, Ann. *See* McCoy, Ann Wyeth
Wyeth, Betsy James, 53–54, *56*, 57–58, *59*, 60, 62,
 63, 66, 70, 72, 74, 78, 94, 96
Wyeth, Carol Bockius, 16, 19, 20, 23, 28, 93
Wyeth, Caroline Pyle, 62
Wyeth, Carolyn, 6, 20, 22, *32*, 33, 40, 42, 44, 66,
 74, 76, 93–94
Wyeth, Edwin, 8
Wyeth, Henriette. *See* Hurd, Henriette Wyeth
Wyeth, Howard Pyle, 62
Wyeth, Jamie (James). *See also individual artworks*
 Andrew's relationship with, 76, 78, 94, 98
 birth of, 66
 childhood of, 6, 66, 72, 74
 early art of, 72, *73*, 74, 76, 77
 in the military, 82
 photograph of, *100*
 portrait of, 66, *67*
 on Southern Island, 96
Wyeth, Nathaniel, 8, 23, 30, *32*, 33, 35, 36, 40,
 60, 62
Wyeth, N.C. (Newell Convers). *See also individual*
 artworks
 Andrew's relationship with, 35, 42, 44–48, 50,
  58, 60, 63, 66
 birth of, 8
 childhood of, 8
 death of, 63
 education of, 10–12, 14–15, 18
 family life of, 6, 20, 23, 24, 26, 28, 33, 38, 40
 marries Carol Bockius, 19
 photographs of, *17*, *46*, *100*
 studio of, 72, 93
Wyeth, Newell Convers, II, 62–63
Wyeth, Nicholas, 62, 66, 74, 94
Wyeth, Phyllis Mills, 82, *84*
Wyeth, Stimson, 8